ANIMAL ATTACK!

Hunting with WOLVES

By Alphia Gangemi

Gareth Stevens
Publishing

Please visit our website, www.garethstevens.com. For a free color catalog of all our high-quality books, call toll free 1-800-542-2595 or fax 1-877-542-2596.

Library of Congress Cataloging-in-Publication Data

Gangemi, Alphia.
 Hunting with wolves / Alphia Gangemi.
     p. cm. — (Animal attack!)
 Includes index.
 ISBN 978-1-4339-7084-9 (pbk.)
 ISBN 978-1-4339-7085-6 (6-pack)
 ISBN 978-1-4339-7083-2 (library binding)
 1. Wolves—Juvenile literature. 2. Predatory animals—Juvenile literature. I. Title.
 QL737.C22G366 2013
 599.77—dc23

                              2012007980

First Edition

Published in 2013 by
Gareth Stevens Publishing
111 East 14th Street, Suite 349
New York, NY 10003

Designer: Katelyn E. Reynolds
Editor: Greg Roza

Photo credits: Cover, p. 1, (cover, pp. 1, 3–24 background image) PHOTO 24/Brand X Pictures/Getty Images; cover, pp. 1, 3–24 (background graphic) pashabo/Shutterstock.com; cover, pp. 4–23 (splatter graphic) jgl247/Shutterstock.com; p. 5 Martin Harvey/Gallo Images/Getty Images; p. 6 Ron Hilton/Shutterstock.com; p. 7 Design Pics/Thinkstock.com; p. 9 Norbert Rosing/National Geographic/Getty Images; p. 10 pandapaw/Shutterstock.com; p. 11 Matthew Jacques/Shutterstock.com; pp. 12–13 Radius Images/Getty Images; p. 14 Intraclique LLC/Shutterstock.com; p. 15 iStockphoto/Thinkstock.com; p. 17 Wollertz/Shutterstock.com; pp. 18, 19 Jim and Jamie Dutcher/National Geographic/Getty Images; p. 21 John Moore/ Getty Images.

Printed in the United States of America

CPSIA compliance information: Batch #CS12GS: For further information contact Gareth Stevens, New York, New York at 1-800-542-2595.

CONTENTS

Words in the glossary appear in **bold** type
the first time they are used in the text.

CANIS

Wolves belong to a scientific group called *Canis*. This group also includes coyotes, jackals, dogs, and **dingos**. There are three species, or kinds, of wolves—*Canis lupus* (gray wolves), *Canis rufus* (red wolves), and *Canis simensis* (Ethiopian wolves).

Of the three species, *Canis lupus* has the most members. There are about 26 **subspecies** within *Canis lupus*. The most common subspecies, the Eurasian wolf, is found in many parts of Europe and Asia. Most of the information in this book will focus on gray wolves.

Fact Hunter

The Eurasian wolf is also called the common wolf, or sometimes just the gray wolf. Its scientific name is *Canis lupus lupus*.

Most of the scientific names shown here come from Latin words. *Canis* means "dog." *Lupus* means "wolf." *Rufus* means "red." However, "simensis" comes from the Semien Mountains in Ethiopia.

Ethiopian wolves

WOLF PACKS

Unlike some wild animals, wolves are highly social. They live in groups called packs that may have more than 30 members. A **dominant** male wolf called the alpha male leads the pack. The pack is made up of the alpha male's **mate**—or alpha female—and their young. Unrelated males may also join a pack.

Altogether, a wolf pack is a dangerous hunting machine. These clever **predators** work together to chase down **prey** and kill it.

Each wolf in a pack has a rank. The alpha male and female are the leaders. The lower a wolf's rank, the longer it must wait to eat after a kill.

Wolves communicate, or talk, in many different ways. They howl, bark, growl, and whine. They also use their bodies and faces to communicate.

HUNTING GROUNDS

Wolves live in all **habitats** north of the **equator** that have enough food to support them. They live in forests, mountains, plains, savannahs, deserts, and the **Arctic**.

A wolf pack's hunting grounds can be as large as 5,000 square miles (13,000 sq km) and as small as 50 square miles (130 sq km). The pack protects this area from other packs. A wolf pack may travel up to 125 miles (200 km) a day while searching for prey.

Fact Hunter

Wolves were once the most widespread mammal in the world. Over the years, people killed wolves to keep livestock safe, reducing their total range by about one-third.

Today, few wolves can be found in Mexico, the United States, and western Europe.

▽

SPOTTING WOLVES

The size of a wolf depends on its species. Those living farther south are generally smaller than those living farther north. Males can weigh between 50 and 175 pounds (23 and 79 kg), but most weigh about 120 pounds (55 kg).

Gray wolves can be gray, brown, black, or reddish. Arctic wolves are completely white. Wolves have long, stiff hairs called guard hairs. In the winter, they grow shorter, softer hairs underneath the guard hairs. These keep them warm when it's cold.

From nose to tail, male wolves can be between 34 and 51 inches (86 and 130 cm) long. Females are a little smaller than males.

The Arctic wolf's coloring helps it blend in with its surroundings. This makes it easier for the wolf to hide while stalking its prey.

BUILT FOR SPEED

Wolves are fast and **agile**. Their legs are longer and stronger than other members of the *Canis* group. They normally jog at about 5 miles (8 km) an hour, but they can sprint 35 miles (56 km) per hour or faster for short bursts.

Wolves can run long distances without tiring. They can run for as long as 20 minutes while chasing prey for up to 3 miles (4.8 km). They can also run quickly through deep snow.

Fact Hunter

Wolves' front paws are larger than their back paws. Their toes are webbed, which makes them great swimmers.

The sight of a sprinting wolf pack can only mean one thing—they're on the hunt!

13

CLAWS AND FANGS

Wolves have sharp claws, but they don't often use them to attack prey. A wolf's claws grip the ground when it moves, allowing the predator to run faster and jump farther when hunting.

A wolf's teeth, on the other hand, are deadly weapons. Wolves have four pointy fangs for grasping and holding onto prey. Between their fangs, wolves have flat, sharp teeth for slicing flesh. Their back teeth are flat and broad, which makes them perfect for grinding up food.

Wolves have greater jaw strength than other members of the *Canis* group. Their bite is twice as strong as a German shepherd's.

A wolf's fangs—also called canines—can be 2 inches (5 cm) long. Their length allows the predator to hold onto large, strong prey.

WOLF SENSES

Wolves have a great sense of smell. They can smell prey from 1 mile (1.6 km) or more away. Once they catch that scent, they start closing in for the kill. Wolves also use their sense of smell to find out information about other wolves.

Wolves have very good hearing. Scientists believe they can hear up to 10 miles (16 km) away in open areas. Wolf vision is about the same as ours. However, wolves can see better at night than people can.

Fact Hunter

Scientists believe a wolf's sense of smell is up to 100 times more sensitive than a person's.

This gray wolf sniffs the ground while following prey. ▽

PACK ATTACK!

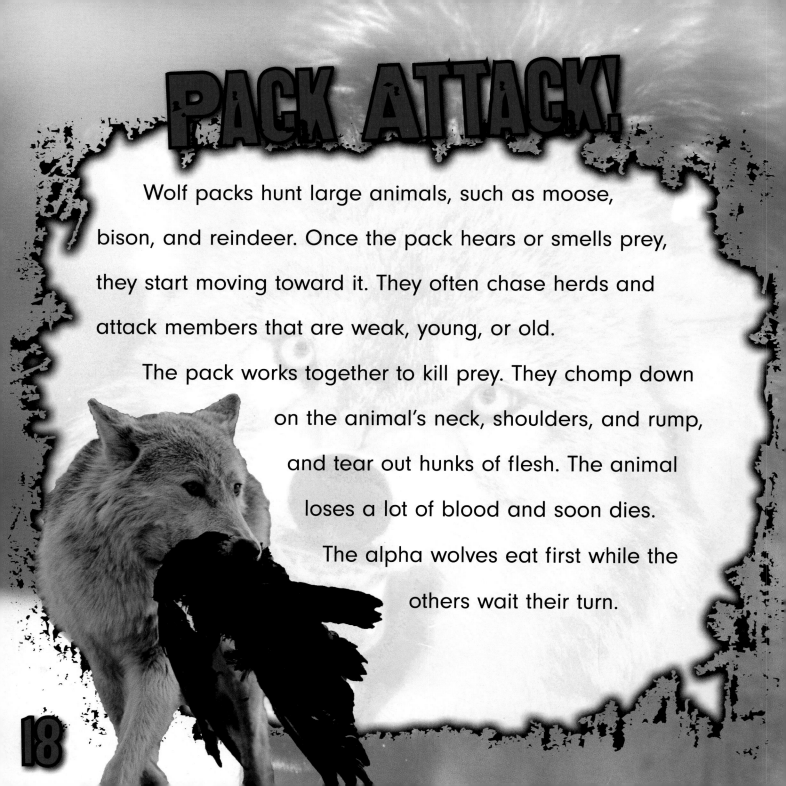

Wolf packs hunt large animals, such as moose, bison, and reindeer. Once the pack hears or smells prey, they start moving toward it. They often chase herds and attack members that are weak, young, or old.

The pack works together to kill prey. They chomp down on the animal's neck, shoulders, and rump, and tear out hunks of flesh. The animal loses a lot of blood and soon dies. The alpha wolves eat first while the others wait their turn.

Single wolves often hunt smaller prey, such as birds, fish, snakes, rabbits, and lizards. A wolf can eat 20 pounds (9 kg) of meat at one time.

Wolves usually won't attack an animal that stands its ground or fights back. They prefer to attack prey that tries to run away.

GRAY WOLVES OF NORTH AMERICA

Gray wolves were once common all over North America. However, they were killed off in great numbers hundreds of years ago. Today, most live in Canada and Alaska. Smaller populations live in Idaho, Michigan, Minnesota, Montana, Wisconsin, and Wyoming. Mexican wolves can be found in New Mexico and Arizona.

Gray wolf populations are growing thanks to the efforts of concerned people. In 1995, 14 wolves from Canada were placed in Yellowstone National Park. Today, there are around 100 wolves in the park. Hopefully their numbers will continue to grow.

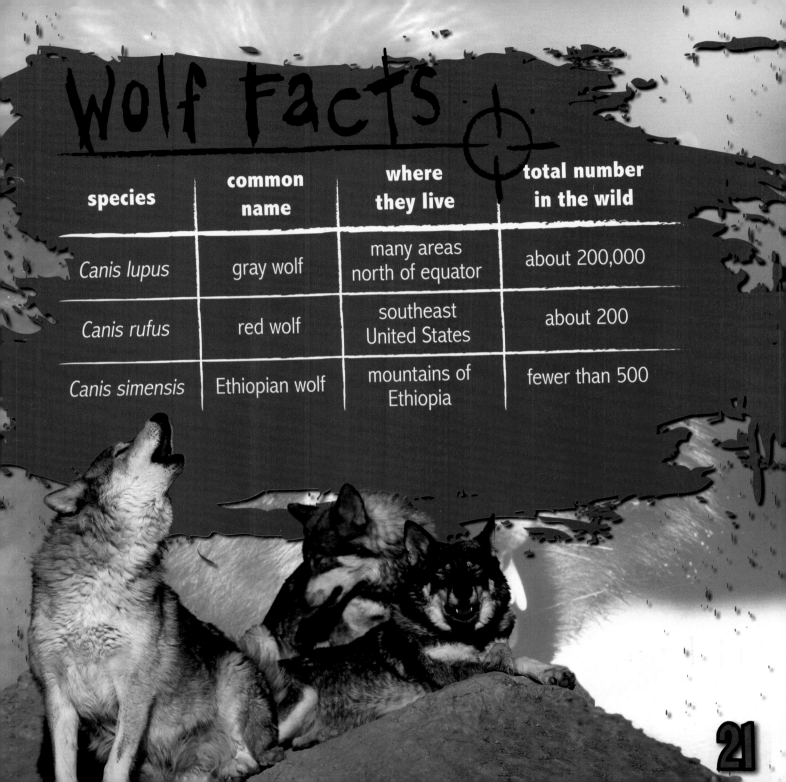

Wolf Facts

species	common name	where they live	total number in the wild
Canis lupus	gray wolf	many areas north of equator	about 200,000
Canis rufus	red wolf	southeast United States	about 200
Canis simensis	Ethiopian wolf	mountains of Ethiopia	fewer than 500

GLOSSARY

agile: able to move quickly and easily

Arctic: the area around the North Pole

dingo: a wild Australian dog with a reddish-brown coat

dominant: the most powerful or strongest; the leader

equator: the imaginary line around Earth that is the same distance from the North and South Poles

habitat: the natural place where a plant or animal lives

mate: one of a pair of animals that come together to make babies

predator: an animal that hunts other animals for food

prey: an animal that is hunted by other animals for food

subspecies: a category of living thing that is a smaller group within a species

FOR MORE INFORMATION

Books

Goldish, Meish. *Gray Wolves: Return to Yellowstone*. New York, NY: Bearport Publishing, 2008.

McLeese, Don. *Gray Wolves*. Vero Beach, FL: Rourke Publishing, 2011.

Slade, Suzanne. *What If There Were No Gray Wolves? A Book About the Temperate Forest Ecosystem*. Mankato, MN: Picture Window Books, 2011.

Websites

Gray Wolves
kids.nationalgeographic.com/kids/animals/creaturefeature/graywolf/
Read more about gray wolves and see pictures of them.

International Wolf Center: Wild Kids
www.wolf.org/wolves/learn/justkids/kids.asp
Learn more about wolves and find some fun wolf projects.

INDEX